Redemption Poems
A Little Book of Remembrance

Rachel Starr Thomson
2020

Redemption Poems: A Little Book of Remembrance

Published by Little Dozen Press
Crystal Beach, ON, Canada
littledozen.com

Copyright © 2020 by Rachel Starr Thomson

Visit the author at rachelstarrthomson.com.

All Rights Reserved. This book, or any portion thereof, may not be reproduced or transmitted in any form or by any means, electronic or mechanical, including photocopying, recording, or by an information storage and retrieval system (except by a reviewer, who may quote brief passages in a review or other endorsement, or in a recommendation to be printed in a magazine, newspaper, or on the Internet) without written permission from the publisher.

ISBN: 978-1-927658-62-8

Redemption Poems

A Little Book of Remembrance

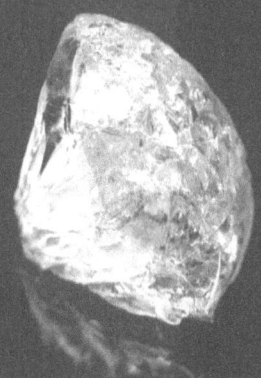

RACHEL STARR
THOMSON

Table of Contents

Introduction	7
Need	9
Hovering	11
Kyrie	13
There Is a Prayer	21
The Closet	23
This Sunday Morning	27
If I Am a Prophet	29

Introduction

This is, as the subtitle indicates, a little book. It contains just seven poems, some very short, some long. They tell the story of salvation on a personal and cosmic level—from our state of lostness and despair ("Need"), to God's rescue mission through Christ ("Kyrie"), to the ways he transforms our lives ("The Closet," "If I Am a Prophet").

The centerpiece is a long poem-prayer called "Kyrie," a meditation on the work of Jesus on the cross.

The pieces in this book were written over a number of years, and most have never been shared anywhere before. ("Kyrie" is the exception: I wrote it for spoken-word performance and gave it at live events across Canada for two years.)

Even as I release *Redemption Poems,* I'm in the process of finishing several larger books—a novel and a volume of scriptural commentary.

Every project is different, of course, and yet it strikes me that I just keep telling the same old story over and over again. The story of forgiveness, incarnation, and redemption. The story of love's victory over sin and death.

It's a beautiful story, and it's true.

We need to be reminded of that, maybe now more than ever.

I hope you enjoy the reflections in these pages. And that they help you remember, today, that the old, old story is still true—and that it, and not our present circumstances, defines the world we live in.

Kyrie eléison.

Rachel

December 2020

NEED

Warm and generous, like the sun

Always giving, ever feeding

The hungers of a world still young

And green and growing, ever needing

Roots that seek and sink down deep

Branches stretched like fingers reaching

To soak up light and drag it down

To hungry hearts that never sleep

And souls forever starving, leeching

Life from air and light and ground.

Soak it up and drag it down

To feed this aching, yawning dark

This ravenous, this hungry ground

This open, empty, grasping heart

I take and take, and still I yearn

To know how fulness feels and see

The Giver smile, and hear him bless

The soil with warmth and peace to learn

To rest in generosity

And full, at last know happiness.

But though he ever gives, yet still

Hungrier I am it seems

With pits and depths and cores to fill,

I am earth, I live, I need.

HOVERING

Hovering. Hovering over an ocean of dark. Still—over the drowning of dreams.

Darkness, the face of the deep.

Something stirs on the water; ripples, faint.

Someone is breathing.

White caps; wind rising.

KYRIE

I.

And God said, Of every tree in the garden you may eat, but of the fruit of the tree of the knowledge of good and evil you may not eat, for in the day that you eat of it you shall surely die.

And we ate, and we knew evil, and we did surely die.

In the day that we ate of it, division.

In the day that we ate of it, strife.

In the day that we ate of it, selfishness.

In the day that we ate of it, pride.

And every day that we sin,

you and I,

we eat again. We know evil by association.

We know good in hints and snatches, by neglect, and by longing.

And in this world of pain and toil,

Of Auschwitz, Rwanda, Killing Fields,

In this world of envy and of hate,

We still feel the wind in the leaves of Eden.

Lord, have mercy.

Kyrie eléison.
Christe eléison.

II.

From Eden to Egypt, our cry remains

Lord, hear us; have mercy;

On thy people Israel, on Pharaoh's slaves.

Have mercy.

III.

Hundreds of years

Books of prophecy, promises of God

Your prophets call us home, though still we wander

Far from mercy, far from You.

Hundreds of years.

Books of prophecy.

Moses, Isaiah, freedom, bondage,

Needing always, every night, every day,

Needing—

Needing You.

Needing mercy,

not just some intangible idea,

not just a pardon on a heavenly scroll.

Needing a hand we can hold.

Needing to walk as we did in the garden.

And God said, "A virgin shall conceive, and shall bring forth a Son.

And you shall call His name Immanuel, for He shall free His people from their sins.

And you shall call Him God

With us."

Lord, have mercy. Christ, have mercy.

Kyrie eléison.

Christe eléison.

IV.

Jesus' hands heal

We touch your mercy.

He opens the way,

We see your mercy.

He is your mercy

He is your grace

Walking among us, a life-giving tree

Tree of good, not of evil.

Trees . . .

One tree still awaits,

One tree still to make its mark.

One branch slashing across a bloody trunk.

Unholy tree, knowledge of evil.

For we ate,

We knew good and evil,

And God Himself will surely die.

V.

And God said, of every tree in the garden you may eat, but of the fruit of the tree of the knowledge of good and evil you may not eat, for in the day that you eat of it, you shall surely die.

And it was as God said it would be.

And God climbed the tree and cried, It is finished.

And God said, Believe.

And God said, Mercy I give you.

I give you forgiveness

Earned at an awesome price.

Welcome, children, to the garden.

Welcome home.

> *Kyrie eléison.*
> *Christe eléison.*

Kyrie Eléison. The words are Greek and mean "Lord, have mercy"; they've been sung by Christians the world over since the earliest centuries of the church. The Kyrie, which is usually sung in threes as an allusion to the Trinity, perfectly expresses the central need of mankind. The Bible declares that "there is none righteous, no, not one," and that because of our personal failure to live as we should, we are eternally separated from our Creator and Judge.

But God has offered us mercy in the person of His Son. Paul tells us that Jesus "was delivered to death for our offences, and raised again for our justification"—to cleanse us before God and place us back into relationship with Him.

On our part, God asks that we turn from our sin and attempts to live without Him, trust in the blood of His Son to cleanse us from all unrighteousness, and go on to live by grace—in relationship with our Father in heaven.

Jesus said, "And this is eternal life, that they may know you the only true God, and Jesus Christ whom you have sent." In the end, that is what *Kyrie eléison* is all about: knowing God because God wants us to know Him; loving Him because He first loved us.

THERE IS A PRAYER

There is a prayer

A prayer in me for breathing

Breathing full and deep and long

Breathing wind and breathing song

Before the rise and fall grows still

The warmth cold, the sound

—.

THE CLOSET

Here I sit

In my deep dark closet

Where the plaster peels

And reveals

Wallpaper that was ugly when they put it up

And is even worse now.

Here I sit

Wishing

For wind in my sails (I dream of sails)

I'd leave

But I'm hung up on all the nails.

Jesus, help me renovate

You pick the paint, I'll spread it

We'll pull off the paper!

Down with plaster!

Give me a hammer

We'll pull all the nails.

Silly child . . .

Come out.

But Jesus, we've not fixed it yet!

And it's not so terribly bad.

The walls will look great in yellow

There are ways to clean up mold

We'll pull out the nails or pound 'em in

New plaster, no rust—

Child, get out of the closet!

Get *out* of the whole rotting *house*.

You can't fix death.

Get out.

But Lord—oh fine, I'm coming.

But I still think—

Oh.

What *is* that?

That, my child, is sky,

Stretched over a green world,

Alight with a million stars,

Windows to heavens beyond,

Pulsing with song and with breath.

It's . . . so much.

Yes.

When I said you would live,

When I said "All things new,"

When I said you would be free,

I didn't mean the closet.

I meant this.

THIS SUNDAY MORNING

This Sunday morning I am alive

And that is a miracle.

I breathe; my hearts beats;

Miracle upon miracle.

This Sunday morning I think, I feel, I speak;

Miracle upon miracle upon miracle.

One Sunday morning you were dead

And that was *catastrophe*.

God unbreathing—

God-heart unbeating—

Catastrophe, chaos, the end.

Dawn . . .

That Sunday morning you came alive,

And that is a *fact*.

You breathed . . . and I breathed!

And that is a miracle!

Alive to God! Raised with you!

Dead to sin and dead to death,

Miracle upon miracle upon miracle!

Twice alive, amazing grace.

Miracle upon miracle.

IF I AM A PROPHET

If I am a prophet

Give me a message

Give me words, and I will speak them

That which I see not, teach thou me

Infuse my mind with meaning.

Words of God, kindling wisdom,

Burn away nonsense, confusion, and fear.

If I am a prophet, invest me with power

Fill me with love, and make my mind clear.

Lift me out

Of this world of my making.

Lift me up

From the noise and the clouds.

If I am a prophet,

Make me a message.

Make me words, and speak them aloud.

Rachel would love to hear from you!

You can visit her and interact online:
Web: www.rachelstarrthomson.com
Facebook.com/RachelStarrThomsonWriter
Twitter: @writerstarr

FEARLESS

You can live free from fear.

Fear steals our lives from us. It steals our impact and cripples our joy.

In our modern world, there are a million reasons to be afraid.

But what if your default mode was courage and faith, not fear and timidity?

True freedom is possible—through the presence of Jesus and the practice of his Word.

In this book, we expose the insidious roots of fear and explore the answers found in the Bible. Learn how:

- THE FEAR OF THE LORD WILL BREAK THE POWER OF LESSER FEARS

- HOLINESS WILL CHANGE YOUR IDENTITY—AND GIVE YOU COURAGE TO STAND AGAINST THE TIDE

- THE PRESENCE OF GOD IS THE ANSWER TO THE WORLD'S TROUBLES

- YOU CAN PRACTICE THE GIFTS OF POWER, LOVE, AND A SOUND MIND

Available from Amazon and everywhere books are sold.

HEART TO HEART

"Father."

With a single word, Jesus Christ ushered His disciples into a new relationship with their Creator. With a single prayer, He opened a door into the heart of God and called men and women to walk through it. In this highly engaging and personal work, Rachel Starr Thomson takes readers on a journey through the most powerful prayer of all time—straight to the heart of the Father.

> *"One of the best things on Jesus' prayer I have read . . . a true devotional experience. A significant contribution to the devotional literature on the Lord's Prayer."*
>
> **—Michael Phillips, Bestselling Author**

> *"A book I'll return to the next time my prayers seem dry and profitless . . . a drink of cool, refreshing water in a parched and thirsty land."*
>
> **—Jean Hall, Eclectic Homeschool Online**

Available from Amazon and everywhere books are sold.

"And I will raise me up a faithful priest, that shall do according to that which is in mine heart and in my mind . . ."

What the world needs is more of Jesus, and it will see more of him when we love him more–know him better–believe and trust in him with all our hearts. This collection of essays is specially written for God's "Samuel Generation": every believer who wishes to know and do the heart and mind of their Father in heaven. In a highly personal and encouraging style, they bring a fresh and convicting look at topics such as grace, love, trusting in dark times, Christian unity, and the character of Jesus Christ.

> *"Letters to a Samuel Generation keeps a balance in building faith, yet acknowledging pain. Calling to action, yet reminding people that doing comes out of BEing. And calling for unity, while still stressing the need to stand for truth."*
>
> **—Mercy Hope, Author and Speaker**
>
> *"To your description of what God's practical love is, my spirit shouted a resounding 'yes!'"*
>
> **—Robin Gilman, Homeschooling Mother of 10**

You can find all of these on Rachel's website at
www.rachelstarrthomson.com/nonfiction

THE SEVENTH WORLD TRILOGY

For five hundred years the Seventh World has been ruled by a tyrannical empire—and the mysterious Order of the Spider that hides in its shadow. History and truth are deliberately buried, the beauty and treachery of the past remembered only by wandering Gypsies, persecuted scholars, and a few unusual seekers. But the past matters, as Maggie Sheffield soon finds out. It matters because its forces will soon return and claim lordship over her world, for good or evil.

The Seventh World Trilogy is an epic fantasy, beautiful, terrifying, pointing to the realities just beyond the world we see.

"An excellent read, solidly recommended for fantasy readers."
– MIDWEST BOOK REVIEW

"A wonderfully realistic fantasy world. Recommended."
– JILL WILLIAMSON, CHRISTY-AWARD-WINNING AUTHOR
OF *BY DARKNESS HID*

"Epic, beautiful, well-written fantasy that sings of Christian truth."
– RAEL, READER

Available everywhere online or special order from your local bookstore.

THE ONENESS CYCLE

The supernatural entity called the Oneness holds the world together. *What happens if it falls apart?*

In a world where the Oneness exists, nothing looks the same. Dead men walk. Demons prowl the air. Old friends peel back their mundane masks and prove as supernatural as angels. But after centuries of battling demons and the corrupting powers of the world, the Oneness is under a new threat—its greatest threat. Because this time, the threat comes from within.

Fast-paced contemporary fantasy.

"Plot twists and lots of edge-of-your-seat action,
I had a hard time putting it down!"
—Alexis

"Finally! The kind of fiction I've been waiting for my whole life!"
—Mercy Hope, FaithTalks.com

"I sped through this short, fast-paced novel, pleased by the well-drawn characters and the surprising plot. Thomson has done a great job of portraying difficult emotional journeys . . . Read it!"
—Phyllis Wheeler, The Christian Fantasy Review

Available everywhere online or special order from your local bookstore.

TIME TO ALIGN:
FREE EMAIL COURSE

Join Rachel Starr Thomson and the 1:11 team for a personal journey through 8 key areas of life in our free email-based course, "Time to Align."

This free, 11-week course is a spiritual recalibration: a chance to bring your heart, soul, mind, and strength into alignment with the nature and will of God.

To get your first lesson straight to your inbox, sign up here:
One11Ministries.com/Align

www.ingramcontent.com/pod-product-compliance
Lightning Source LLC
LaVergne TN
LVHW040203080526
838202LV00042B/3300